My Community

Elaine Cowan

Lecturer in Social Subjects, Faculty of Education, University of Aberdeen

General Editor

Liz Clark

Postgraduate Primary Programme Director, Faculty of Education, University of Aberdeen

Illustrated by Jane Ryan

Published and typeset by
Pulse Publications
Braehead, Stewarton Road, by Kilmaurs, Ayrshire,
KA3 2NH

Printed and bound by
Thomson Colour Printers

British Library Cataloguing-in-Publication Data
A Catalogue record for this book is available from
the British Library
ISBN 0 948 766 91 3
© Cowan 2003 (Text)
© Pulse Publications 2003 (Family illustrations)

Introduction

The series **People in Society: Citizenship in Action** provides pupils in the middle and upper stages of primary schools with a meaningful introduction to many of the important issues facing young people as citizens in society today. This series will encourage children to analyse and debate a range of issues and information related to **Education for Citizenship** in order to develop knowledge, understanding, skills, values and creative abilities, enabling them to participate fully as active and responsible citizens.

The series is built around a conceptual framework. Through the activities included in the books, pupils will develop:

● understanding of:
  – people and their needs
  – rules, rights and responsibilities in society
  – conflict and decision making locally, nationally and globally;

● skills related to preparing for, carrying out, and reviewing and reporting on enquiry tasks;

● informed attitudes on respect and care for self and others and on social and environmental responsibility.

Pupils will be supported through studying familiar situations and contemporary issues. They will be encouraged to examine social and related moral issues and dilemmas through a range of activities including questions, discussion, debates and case studies that require the collection, use and evaluation of evidence.

Contents

This new series covers the outcomes and attainment targets for the **National Guidelines People in Society 5–14** for pupils working towards Levels C/D in Scotland and a range of activities appropriate for **Key Stage 2 Citizenship** in England and Wales.

Summary of the main 5-14 People in Society KU/ES Strands and Attainment Targets and Aspects of Citizenship included in this book.

5-14 People in Society

KU strands	Level C	Level D
People and Needs in Society	1.1, 1.2	1.1, 1.3
Rules, Rights and Responsibilities	2.1, 2.2	2.2, 2.3
Conflict and Participation in Decision Making	3.1	3.1

Skills (for enquiry)		
Planning for tasks	1.2	1.2
Carrying out tasks	2.1, 2.2	2.1, 2.2
Reviewing and Reporting on tasks	3.1, 3.2	3.1, 3.2

Developing Informed Attitudes – Positive Attitudes and Awareness of:

Respect and care for others	2.1
Social and environmental responsibility	2.2, 3.1, 3.2, 3.5

Education for Citizenship
Themselves and the world in which they live
Legal and human rights and responsibilities of citizens
Sources of disagreement/conflict and the ways people can resolve them
Core skills (communication, Numeracy, ICT, Working with Others, Problem Solving)
Generic skills
(e.g. Decision making, Imaginative responses to issues, Consider perspectives of others)

Citizenship QCA Level 2
Taking part – developing skills of communication and participation
Choices
Children's Rights – human rights
How do rules and laws affect me?
Local democracy for young citizens

Needs in the Community

Outcomes

By the end of this section you should know:

- what the needs and wants of a family are

- what the needs in a community are

- how to carry out some basic enquiry tasks.

Wordfile

Needs: things a person must have to live (e.g. food, shelter, warmth). These are also called necessities.

Wants: things that are not essential but having them improves the way we live (e.g. a car or a television). These are sometimes also called luxuries.

Meet the MacKay Family
The MacKay family lives in Green Street, Linview in Scotland. Jack and Helen and their two children, Anna (12) and Scott (10), live together in their house. Two years ago Sadie (Helen's mother) moved in to live with them.

I've lived here all my life and I've worked at the textile factory since I left school. It's so close to our house, I just walk to work each day. At weekends, I enjoy watching the Rovers team during the football season, especially if they win. It would be nice to have a car to go to away matches. I used to do a lot of fishing but I don't have the time now. I like bowls and have a game whenever I can.

I like living here. Our house overlooks the park. Most people are very friendly and chat with me when they pop into the baker's shop where I work. When I'm not at work, I'm busy looking after the kids and Mum now too. I like to go out to the pictures in Dundon each week with my pal, Lisa. If only we could have a holiday. We haven't had one for more than five years.

I moved down to live with Helen, my daughter, two years ago when my husband, Tom, died. I'd like to go back more often to the meetings at 'the Rural' in my old village to see my old chums but I'm finding it hard to get about. I need a new hip so I can't walk far. Still, I've a nice room looking out over the park. If only Jack had a car or the buses were better here.

I enjoy football and go with Dad to the Rovers' home matches. I ride my bike or go skateboarding in the park with my pals whenever Mum lets me. Still, I wish I had a computer so I could play games, and the internet would be good for my homework! I'm always hungry. Mum says I have 'hollow legs'.

Activities

1. Write a sentence in your own words to explain each of the following: **Needs Wants**

2. Draw up a table like the one below using the earlier information about the members of the MacKay family.

    For each member of the MacKay family, complete the table to identify their main needs and wants.

Person	Needs	Wants
Jack		
Helen		A holiday
Anna		
Scott		
Sadie	A new hip	

Linview's OK.
I moved up to the High School this year. There are lots more people to make friends with and all sorts of clubs and groups to join. There's not a lot to do here. I go to the Youth Club on Saturday but we wish we could get to the cinema more or 10 pin bowling. They're miles away and we can't always afford the bus fares.

Linview–A Local Community

Linview is a small town in eastern Scotland. Only about 8,000 people live there. Most people work in the local textile factory or in the other small businesses in the town such as the shops and hotels. Some people work to provide services for local people such as the doctors at the health centre and teachers and other staff in the schools.

A few years ago, a new housing estate was built on the edge of town. This provided housing that attracted people who work mainly in Dundon, the big town ten miles away. They travel by car and bus to work each day but their children go to Linview's primary and secondary schools. No new employers have come to the area in recent years so some people have been unable to find work in the town.

Activities

1. Look at all the information on the town of Linview.

   Draw up two lists:
   – things that would make you want to live in Linview
   – things you would want to change about Linview.

2. For one of the things you would change about Linview, suggest how this would make Linview a better place to live.

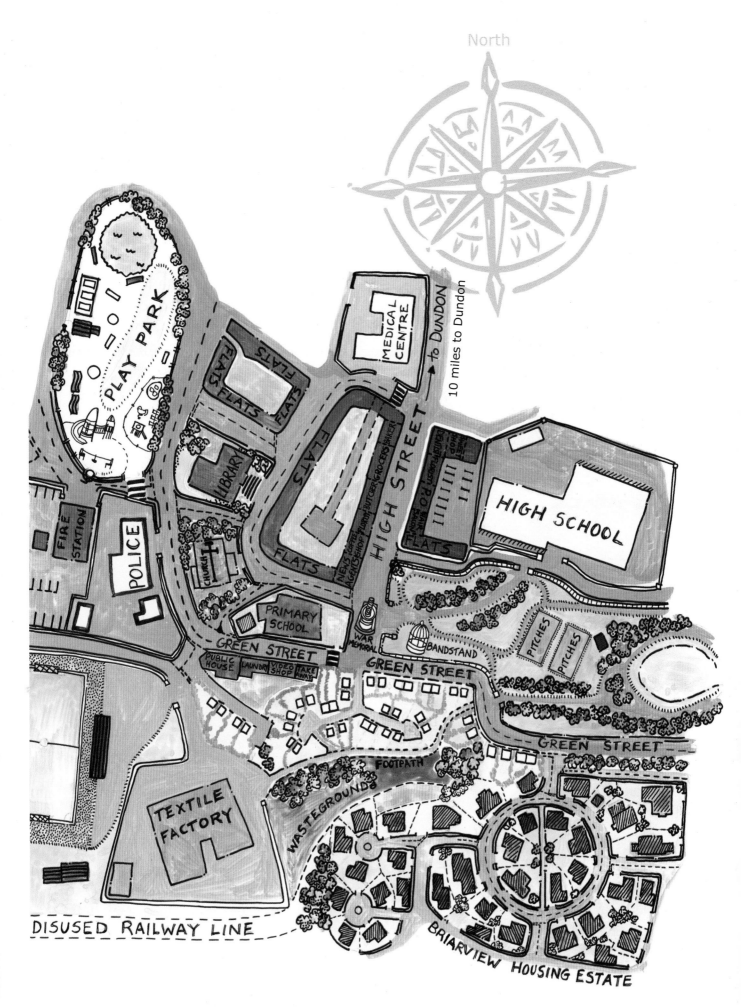

Needs in Society: The After School Club

As Anna said, there's not a lot for young people to do in Linview. To go to the cinema or bowling they need to catch a bus into Dundon.

The local police are worried that some young people might get into trouble if they are bored. They could cause a nuisance to other people in the community, hanging around on street corners in large groups.

A new scheme has started, making money available for after school clubs. Some teachers from the local school think it would be a good idea for Linview to have one too. A club will help pupils with their homework and let them make use of some of the other facilities in the school such as the computers and the gym.

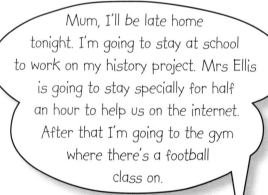

Mum, I'll be late home tonight. I'm going to stay at school to work on my history project. Mrs Ellis is going to stay specially for half an hour to help us on the internet. After that I'm going to the gym where there's a football class on.

What a good idea this club is. It gives you so much more to do. You can stay with your friends and get help to do your homework too.

At the High School, we're going to have a club also. We'll be able to use the computers and there'll be dance classes and games as well.

That's good and it also helps parents who work in Dundon. They're able to collect their children later than the normal school finishing time.

In my day we wouldn't have stayed late at school for anything.

That's not true. You used to stay for football training and go in to play on Saturdays too.

That's right Helen, you tell him.

 **Activities:**

1. What is an after school club?

2. In what ways does it help the parents and children in the local area?

3. Does your school have an after school club? If so, find out
   - who runs it;
   - what times it is open until;
   - what activities children can do there;
   - if it is busy or not.

   Do you ever go to it?

If your school does not have one, can you find out about one near you?

Needs in Society: Sadie's Lunch Club

Several days each week, Sadie goes to a lunch club in Linview. The club is held in an old church on the main street, converted and adapted to meet the needs of, for example, people in wheelchairs. This club is one way Sadie has made new friends since moving to Linview. The programme for one week in January is given below:

Weekly Programme
14–18 January

Monday 14th

10–12	Carpet bowls
12.30	Lunch
1.30–3.30	Jigsaw club

Lunch menu – mince and potatoes

Tuesday 15th

10.30–11.30	Over 50s keep fit
12.30	Lunch
1.30	Speaker from Dundon College: 'Eat 5 for life' – healthy menus on a pension

Lunch menu – lasagne and salad

Wednesday 16th

10–12	Carpet Bowls
12.30	Lunch
1.30–3.30	Discussion group followed by weekly worship (this week's chaplain: Father Hobbs, St David's Church)

Lunch menu – steak pie and chips

Thursday 17th

10.30–11.30	Over 50s keep fit
12.30	Lunch
1.30–3.30	Alice Larbert: Travels in Oz

Lunch menu – chicken casserole

Friday 18th

10–12	Questions about benefits Visitor from Dundon Citizens Advice Bureau
12.30	Lunch
1.30–5.30	Dundon theatre matinee

Lunch menu – fish and chips

SOURCE 1

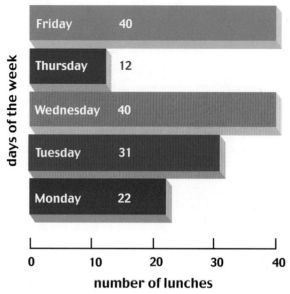

Lunches served each day

Day	number of lunches
Friday	40
Thursday	12
Wednesday	40
Tuesday	31
Monday	22

days of the week

number of lunches

SOURCE 2

Ages of people attending club

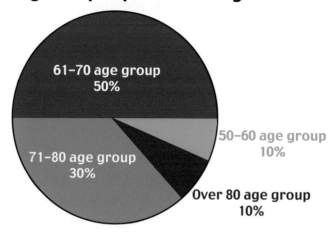

61–70 age group 50%

50–60 age group 10%

71–80 age group 30%

Over 80 age group 10%

SOURCE 3

Two minibuses took 20 people to the theatre on Friday afternoon.

 **Activities:**

Look at the programme and the information in the graph and pie chart above about attendance at the lunch club.

1. Do you agree with Sadie? Is there a variety of things to do in the lunch club programme?

2. Which groups of people do you think the activities of the lunch club were aimed at? Give evidence for your view.

3. Which activities were the most popular at the lunch club that week? Give evidence for your view.

4. Would you agree that the lunch club programme meets the needs of the elderly in Linview? Explain your view using examples from the information about the club.

It's the variety of things to do that makes the club so popular. The lunches are good and there's always time for a chat and a joke. It's a good way to make friends.

Needs in Society: **They're Closing our Library**

Wordfile

Councillor: a person elected to the council to speak for the local people.

Community council: a group of people chosen locally to discuss suggestions on many local issues.

Council: a group of people elected to take decisions affecting the local area on services (such as education and libraries) and on planning for roads and houses.

Petition: a letter people sign (usually as a protest) stating their views on an issue. They send it off to the council or government to try to influence a decision.

Councillor Anderson put up a notice in the shop window last week about the new library. We've had leaflets in the shop all week. I'd like to go to the meeting.

Community Council Meeting
7.30 Tuesday 26 October
in Church Hall

Come along to the meeting on 26 October and find out more about the plans for a new library in Dundon to replace the 1894 library building. Councillors Anderson and Hamilton will be on hand to explain how the new library service will work and what it will mean for all the people of Linview into the 21st Century.

Why do we need a new library? I don't want to have to travel 10 miles to Dundon just to borrow a book!

Mrs Edwards, at school, was saying the new library will have lots of things apart from books. There'll be games, CD-ROMs and videos to borrow. The reference library will have computers and the Internet as well to use for free.

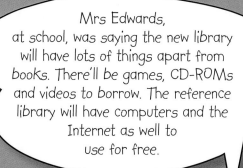

... it'll mean we can find out about topics like local history by using newspapers, books and even computers when we're doing projects at school. It'll help us do our homework and learn in a modern way.

Most people at the lunch club don't want the library to close. As it's here in town, many of us use it. If this goes through, all we're going to have in Linview is a library van two days each month. We've signed a petition to send to the council to make sure it stays open.

**Activities:**

Using all the information, answer the questions below.

1. Who is planning the new library?

2. What facilities will it have?

3. How have people in Linview found out about the plans for the library?

4. Summarise the following information in a table:

People in favour of the new library	Reasons they give for being in favour	People against the new library	Reasons they give for being against

5. How have some people from Linview passed on their views to the council about the plans?

6. Imagine you are Councillor Anderson or one of the experts who work for the council.

   Suggest what you might say at the meeting to win more people in Linview over to your point of view.

7. What do you think? Is the new library a good idea or not?
   Give reasons for your view.

Needs in Society: Sadie's Sore Hip

Although Sadie is only 66, she is having trouble walking. The local doctor says she is generally very fit. However, she needs an operation to give her a new artificial hip joint so that she can walk about again without pain.

Sadie has been waiting for five months to see the surgeon at the hospital in Dundon. Finally, a letter comes from the hospital arranging an appointment. As the MacKays have no car, the hospital has arranged for an ambulance to collect Sadie on the day of her appointment and to drop her back home later.

During the appointment, Sadie has X-rays and lots of other tests. The doctor then explains that there is a waiting list for the operation which she needs. Sadie will probably have to wait another six months before she will be called back to the hospital for the operation. She feels quite upset as she had not realised she would still have to wait in pain for a long time.

Sadie picks up a leaflet in the waiting room. It is full of facts and figures about the hospital. She can see that lots of other people are having to wait too. A new hospital is planned for Dundon with new facilities and more beds. The leaflet explains that it is a shortage of doctors and nurses that is really causing delays for patients.

Later, when she gets home, Sadie shows the leaflet to the family. Helen is angry that her mother has to have a further wait for the operation after already waiting so long for the initial appointment at the hospital.

Dundon
hospital needs you

Are you a former health care worker? Did you train as a nurse, radiographer, laboratory technician, medical secretary?

Did you leave the NHS to care for your family? Would you be ready now to do a job that helps people in your area? We offer refresher courses, retraining, a staff creche and nursery, and family–friendly working hours.

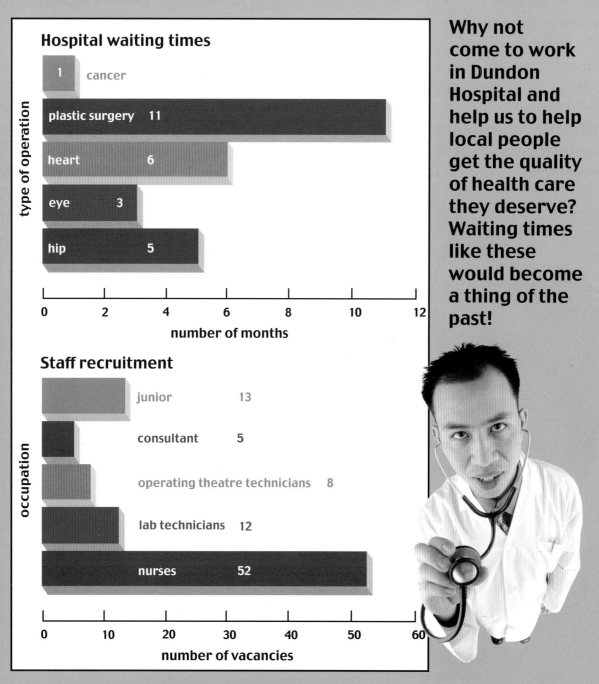

Hospital waiting times

type of operation

cancer	1
plastic surgery	11
heart	6
eye	3
hip	5

number of months (0 2 4 6 8 10 12)

Staff recruitment

occupation

junior	13
consultant	5
operating theatre technicians	8
lab technicians	12
nurses	52

number of vacancies (0 10 20 30 40 50 60)

Why not come to work in Dundon Hospital and help us to help local people get the quality of health care they deserve? Waiting times like these would become a thing of the past!

For further information on our 'Return to Work' programme and the ways we can help you with retraining and childcare, call Louise on Health Professionals hotline

08001237398

 Activities

1. How long **in total** will Sadie have had to wait before she finally gets the hip operation she needs?

2. Look at the bar graph in the leaflet that Sadie picked up at the hospital. Which ailments have
   (i) the longest and
   (ii) the shortest waiting times?

3.

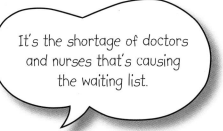

It's the shortage of doctors and nurses that's causing the waiting list.

Does the table on staff shortages in the hospital leaflet back up the doctor's statement or not?
Explain your answer.

4. Imagine you are Helen.
   Use the information about Sadie and the information from the leaflet. Write a letter to the local newspaper. In the letter explain why you are angry about Sadie's long wait for her operation.

Dear Editor...

Conflict and Decision Making

Outcomes

By the end of this section, you should know:

- that decisions are often taken by representatives

- that groups have conflicting views on decisions

- how to use enquiry skills to find out answers.

Wordfile

Representative: someone who speaks for you.

Election: when people vote for their representatives.

Secret Ballot: votes cast in private so no one else will know for whom you voted (usually a written vote).

Who speaks for us?

Scott's school was visited recently by the national school inspectors. They spent a week watching different classes and talking to staff and pupils about the school. So that everyone will feel that they are part of the school, they suggested that Mr Brown, the Head Teacher, should consult pupils and staff before taking decisions.

Later, he decides to set up a Pupils' Council to give the pupils more say in how the school is run. Each form class is to vote for a representative. The Council will meet for an afternoon twice each month. It will advise Mr Brown on how to make the school a better place for everyone. For example, it might discuss issues such as school uniform, the need for school rules, and how additional money or staff will be used. After each meeting, the representatives are to tell their classes about the issues that the Council is discussing.

At the start of the term, an election will be organised in each class. People who wish to be representatives will volunteer and then a vote by secret ballot will be held in each class.

Activities:

1. Who advised that a Pupils' Council should be set up at the school? What reason was given?

2. Who is to be on it and how are members to be chosen?

3. How often has it to meet?

4. What will it discuss? Do you think this is a good idea?

5. Who do you think would take the final decisions – the Pupils' Council or the Head Teacher, Mr Brown? Why would this be so?

6. Look at the bar graph. Who becomes the representative for Class P6? In what way was that person chosen?

7. Does your school have a Pupils' Council?
   - If yes, find out about how it is chosen, its meetings and what is discussed.
   - If no, find out if your class thinks it would be a good idea. Explain why they think this.
   Does your teacher agree? Explain why he or she feels this way.

Pupils' Council P6

candidates	number of votes
Tom	4
Nesreen	6
John	8
Scott	12

0   2   4   6   8   10   12
number of votes

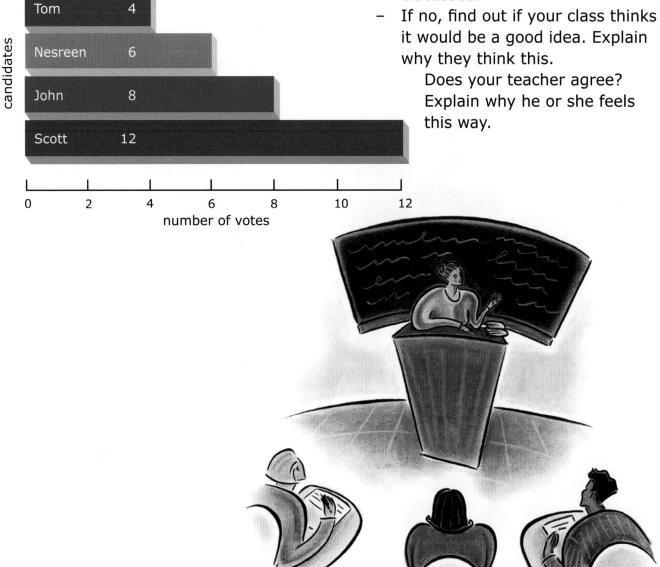

Conflict and Decision Making: The Work of the Pupils' Council

At Scott's school, the Pupils' Council meets for the first time. Among the issues discussed is how to make sure each year group could have an allocated space inside the building during breaks in the winter. It is also decided that all pupils can wear long black trousers at any time of the year.

Another issue discussed is which charity to support at the annual fund raising event – **Children in Need** or **Comic Relief**. Both charities help people in need. To raise the money, pupils would be involved in a range of events from selling fruit and home-made cakes at break to sponsored silences in class.

Children in Need is held each year in late November and mainly helps children in Britain. **Comic Relief** is held once every two years in March. It spends one-third of the money raised on projects abroad, one-third in Britain and one-third specifically on the disabled here and abroad.

The Council is split. Mr Brown suggests that a referendum should be held among all the pupils in the school to help decide on this issue. After a brief one-week campaign in the school, a secret ballot is held in each class.

School Referendum
It's your choice

Our school charity campaign this year – should it be Comic Relief or Children in Need?

Make sure you vote!

 **Wordfile**

Referendum: when everyone votes on a question to help in deciding what to do about an issue.

Campaign: using posters, leaflets or speeches to persuade people to vote for or against an issue.

Charities Referendum Ballot Paper

We work hard each year to raise money for other people who are not so well off.

The Pupils' Council wants you to help decide which charity to help this year.

Please read the question below and tick one box:

In the next year do you want our school to support:

☐ **Children in Need**
☐ **Comic Relief**
☐ **Both equally**
☐ **Neither charity**

Thank you for helping us to decide on this issue.

The referendum results are given in the pie chart below.

Referendum results

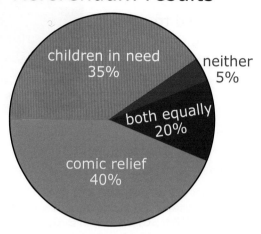

 **Activities:**

Read the information on the Pupils' Council meeting.

1. What issues did the Council consider at its first meeting?

2. Which issue do **you** think was the most important? Give reasons for your answer.

3. When the Council was split over the charity issue, what did it do to help it to make a choice?

4. Do you think this was a good way to decide? Give a reason for your answer.

5. What was the final choice in the school? Explain how you know this.

6. Which would you have chosen? Give reasons for your choice.

Conflict and Decision Making: The Local Community

Just as our health needs are met by the National Health Service, many other people who help us are also said to provide us with 'services'.

 Activities

1. Look back at the earlier map of Linview (on page 7). List all the local services shown on the map.

2. What other services are usually provided in a local community?

Many services in the local community are provided by the local council. Each community has a council made up of councillors. These are people who are elected for each area of the town by voters who are aged 18 and over. Once elected, the councillors represent the people who live in that community, usually for the next four years. These councillors take decisions on how local services will be provided.

The government gives councils most of the money that they need to pay for local services. To top up the money they need, the council collects council tax from local people.

The council takes decisions on lots of local issues. For example, the council decides if a new road is to be built or if you need permission when you want to build an extension to your house. Each council employs a range of experts to advise the councillors on the law and on special issues such as education, roads, and waste disposal.

Read the article below from the local newspaper about the plans the new Dundon Council has for its local area.

The newspaper with all your local news.....   *Friday 5 May*

DUNDON CHRONICLE

50p

The recent election resulted in a new look for our council. Over half of those voted in as councillors are new to the job. The new look is not just in people but also in the policies that the council plans to follow.

Among the changes suggested are:
- a new community high school building
- free swimming for the under-15s
- computers and internet access at a new library in Dundon
- recycling of all cans, bottles and newspapers
- more lunch clubs for the over-60s.

These ideas are fine but where will the money come from? These councillors promised during the election not to put up the council tax. Take a glance at the figures below:

Source of Council's money	Council spending
Government Grant = £161m	Education & Leisure = £200m
Council Tax = £81m	Police, Fire = £35m
Business Rates = £76m	Planning & Environmental Services = £21m
Charges e.g. from rents and entry fees = £44m	Social Work & Housing = £60m
	Transport & Roads = £40m
	Other = £1m

All this costs £1570 for every person living in the area each year. Even without the new promises, all the money has already been spent!

Activities

1. Write a few sentences to describe the way councillors are chosen for their local area.

2. Look carefully at the newspaper article. Is the writer correct to state that "all the money's already been spent"? Give reasons to support your view.

3. Choose one of the five new promises listed in the article:
   - Why do you think this is important for the local community?
   - Who will benefit?
   - Will it be expensive to introduce?

4. In your class, you are going to hold a debate to decide which of the planned policies the council should introduce.

   - You may need to do research from elsewhere in Britain by using real newspaper stories (e.g. from the internet) to gather some facts and figures about similar projects. Most local councils have a website with information on their spending and policies e.g. www.aberdeenshire.gov.uk

   - Write a speech for the debate to justify your choice. Remember you should explain the reasons why you favour this proposal. You will have to give examples to justify your choices. (Examples and relevant information such as facts and figures are all called **evidence**).

   - At the end of the debate, the class will vote to decide which will be the best policy for the council to follow.

Conflict and Decision Making: Planning and People

EXTRA!!! **The Times** EXTRA!!!

New Supermarket for Linview?

Dundon Council Planning Committee debated a planning proposal from a major supermarket chain at its monthly meeting yesterday. The retail giant (as yet unnamed) wants to use most of Victoria Park in Linview as the site for its new store.

Access to the supermarket for out of town traffic would be from the planned bypass around the outskirts of Linview. A new access road into the site would be built along the line of the old railway.

Victoria Park at present is mainly open space and football and other sporting pitches. The money raised would be £5 million for the site plus another million to help with the cost of the bypass. This money would be used to upgrade leisure facilities at the High School. These would include a 'state of the art' swimming pool with a movable floor, a drama studio and 'all weather' pitches for community use for football, hockey and tennis.

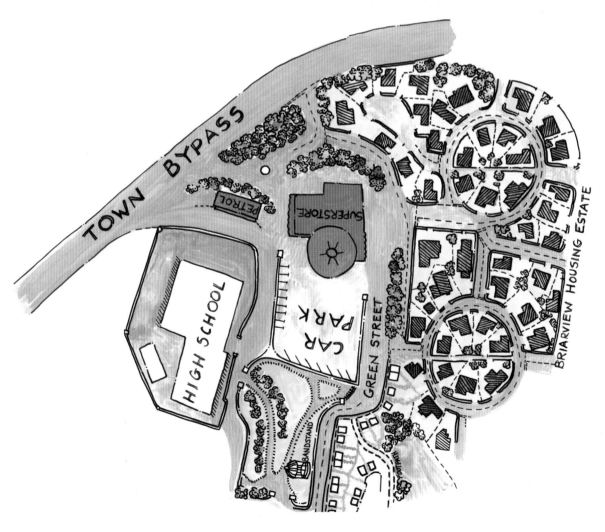

Dear Editor,

When we moved to Linview two years ago, we were promised that the area next to our new homes would be landscaped. Also on all the plans were improved shopping and leisure facilities with a swimming pool in the local area. We demand that these promises are kept. The cash offered for Victoria Park would pay for a lot of badly needed facilities in Linview.

What have we got instead? Next to our houses Victoria Park just has pitches. These are badly drained and covered in water whenever it rains. Next door to the park is a stagnant pond that's full of rubbish. The water is dirty and in hot weather it is covered in green algae and smells. It is a health hazard. In addition, as the pond is not properly fenced, it is a serious danger to our small children.

Yours sincerely,

Jessie Reid
(and 23 others)
Briarview Estate Action Group, Linview

I said it would be a mistake to build houses at Briarview. Look at this. The council wants to build a new supermarket on the park where I played football. Most people in the new estate want the pond drained. That's where I learned to fish. There are all kinds of birds and other wildlife there in the summer and in winter. What do you think we could do to stop them?

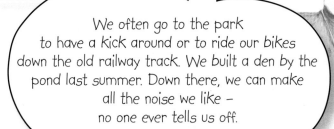

We often go to the park to have a kick around or to ride our bikes down the old railway track. We built a den by the pond last summer. Down there, we can make all the noise we like – no one ever tells us off.

Activities:

Answer the questions below.

1. Where is the supermarket to be built?

2. What other benefits would the development of the site for the supermarket bring to the people of Linview?

3. What disadvantages would there be for people there?

4. Draw up a table for the MacKay family. List, with their reasons, those who are in favour and those who are against the development.

5. Add other groups of people in Linview to the table according to their views of the supermarket development.

6. **Decisions? Decisions?**

   Organise a public meeting to decide on the issue of the new supermarket for Linview.

a. Divide into groups e.g.
   - the residents of the Briarview Estate
   - other residents of Linview
   - people who want to turn the pond into a nature reserve
   - local business people
   - the local councillors
   - Council Planning Department
   - the supermarket's planning team

b. Each group should use the information to develop a short speech for their position in the meeting, giving reasons for their views. In addition, each group should make up questions to ask the other groups.

c. Afterwards, write up a report of the meeting for the local newspaper **or** make a recording for the local radio station of the meeting and the decision taken.

RULES, RIGHTS AND RESPONSIBILITIES

**Outcomes**

By the end of this section you should know:

- your main rights in society

- rights have matching responsibilities for individuals

- how to use enquiry skills to find out answers.

**Wordfile**

Rights: what everyone in society can legally claim (e.g. a fair trial, education from age 5 to age 16, free health care).

Responsibilities: duties we are expected to do (e.g. tell the truth in court, pay our taxes, not break the law).

Rules, Rights and Responsibilities: At Home

1. Did you hear that.? In Wales, school children on average get £8 pocket money each week! Wow!

2. I only get £1 and, since you went to the High School, Anna, you get £2 each week. We need a rise!

3. Think yourselves lucky you get anything. Your bedrooms are always untidy and you never help with the washing up.

4. I never got any pocket money as a lad. I had to earn it with a paper round and then save up for anything I wanted.

5. That was in the 'dark ages' Dad.

Later that day the adults were chatting again about the earlier report on Breakfast TV.

It's a good job the kids didn't stay to hear the rest of that TV report. The lowest amount of pocket money was in Scotland but even that was £4 per week!

I know it's hard for the children, especially Anna. Some of her friends are quite well off but we can't afford lots of pocket money. What if we said they could earn extra by helping around the house?

They should be helping anyway as we both work and Sadie can only do so much with her hip.

I'm fine Jack, really, but what if I help too? I've told you before I can afford to pay a bit more for my keep.

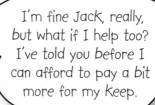

Oh Mum that's good of you but you know we can manage. I suppose we could draw up a list of jobs. We could give them a small amount of money for helping to do each task. Or we could keep a note of what they do each day and at the end of the week add to their pocket money.

Activities

1. Explain the phrase "school children on average get £8 pocket money each week".

2. Draw up a list of tasks around a house that children like Anna and Scott might reasonably help to do.

3. Conduct a survey on pocket money in your class. Ask:

   - how many people get pocket money each week?

   - how much classmates receive each week (e.g. less than £1, between £1 and £2, more than £2)

   - do they have to do extra jobs to get the money?

   - do they save most of their pocket money or spend it all each week?

4. Draw graphs to show the results of your survey.

5. Explain what each graph shows.

Rules, Rights and Responsibilities: **In the Classroom**

Anna enjoys almost everything about her new school. One day she is chatting with Sadie, her Gran, about one subject where some children are causing problems.

We had a new teacher today. She seems very nice and she wears gorgeous clothes. Some of the children in my class just wouldn't listen to what she was saying, Gran.

Maybe it's just because she's new?

No, I don't think so. Some of my class are not interested in the subject and just don't want to work. They say there's no point in learning it.

... but you're all only in first year. How can they know that? Aren't there rules on how they should behave?

Oh yes. Here they are ... in my jotter from Day One. We call them the "Be list"!

It is important in every class in our school to:
- Be respectful of other people and their property (whether visitors, teachers or classmates).
- Be on time for class and ready to start work quickly.
- Be organised. So have everything you need with you for the class – pencil, books, jotters or PE kit.
- Be careful to leave pathways between desks clear of bags and jackets to avoid accidents.
- Be pleasant and good humoured.
- Be attentive and listen carefully so others listen to you.
- Be polite but ask when things are not clear ... but especially be patient, be a friend not a bully.

Give everyone in class a fair chance to do their very best work.

 **Activities**

1. Look over the Linview school rules. Why do you think Anna and her friends call it the "Be list"?

2. Which rule do you think is the most important? Why? Do your classmates agree?

3. Who do you think made up these rules?

4. Why do you think many schools have rules?

5. Do you have rules in your class? If yes, are any of your class rules the same as these? Who made up your school rules?

6. Now suggest three rules that you wish your school or class had. Why do you think each is important? Do your classmates agree with your rules?

7. Make a list of as many laws as you can think of. (Clue: think of laws to do with traffic, property, public safety and how we treat each other.)

8. Which laws are most important to you?

9. Suggest a new law that might be needed.

> Well Anna, they'll find out eventually that in life there are lots of rules. Many, like the ones on your "Be list", are to do with politeness and the way we treat one another. Some are very important and we call these laws. We accept these as they make life easier and safer for everyone ... like laws on speed limits and not driving when drunk or on drugs.
>
> There's no way we could live together today without such laws. New laws are made all the time! Of course, if you break the law, it can be very serious.

10. Log onto **www.parliament.org.uk** or **www.scottishparliament.org.uk** and see which new laws have been made recently in the UK and also in Scotland.

Rules, Rights and Responsibilities: Keeping Safe

The council plans to improve the local playground. Scott's class is going to look around it tomorrow. The children have decided to see what there is for each of the different age groups to do there. They also want to know what people think a good play area should have. Then the class will write to the local paper and the local council with the results of the survey.

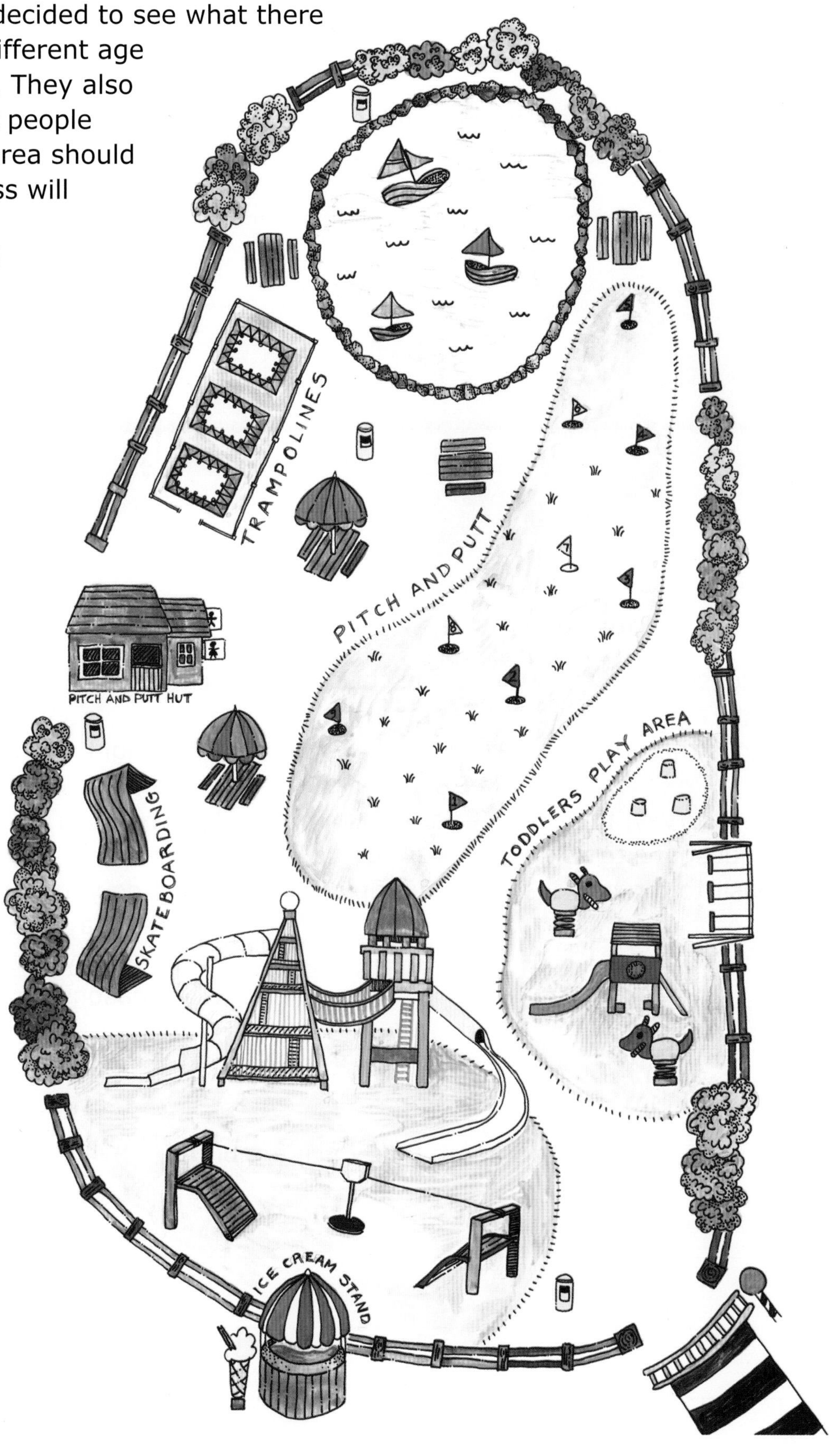

TRAMPOLINES

PITCH AND PUTT

PITCH AND PUTT HUT

SKATE BOARDING

TODDLERS PLAY AREA

ICE CREAM STAND

Activities

1. Identify any dangers the class should discuss before they go to the play park.

2. Suggest three rules the class might make to keep safe.

3. Suggest three other things the class might agree on so that everyone enjoys the time in the park.

For their survey, the class decides on some questions to ask people during their visit to the park. Look at the table below.

4. Write down some other questions they might ask. Try to word the questions so that people can easily reply with a 'yes' or 'no'.

5. The children do their survey on a school day during the week.

a. Why might this not be the best day and time to do this type of survey? Give reasons for your answer.

b. When do you think would be the best day and time to run a survey such as this? Give reasons for this answer.

Questions		
1. Do you visit this park more than once a month?	Yes	No
2. Do you like the park?	Yes	No
3.		
4.		
5.		

6. During the visit, the children asked ten people whether they used the park and what they would like to see there. The results of their survey are given below.

Questions	Yes	No
1. Do you visit the park more than once per month?	IIIII III	II
2. Do you like the park?	IIIII II	III
3. What the park needs:		
– New playground equipment	IIIII III	II
– Paddling pool	IIII	IIIII I
– Skateboard/bike ramp	IIIII II	III
– Cafe	IIIII IIII	I
– Separate area for walking dogs	IIIII IIII	I
– Safer surfaces	IIIII III	II

a. Draw a series of graphs using the survey results.

   – Give each graph a title.

   – Colour code the graphs to show the replies – green for 'yes', red for 'no'.

b. Write a sentence for each graph as a conclusion that sums up what the answers to the question show.

7. Write a letter to the council or to a newspaper giving the conclusions that you made from the survey.

Rules, Rights and Responsibilities: Children's Rights in the UK

Keeping children safe and meeting their needs is very important. In Britain, all children have certain rights. For example:

- all children get free health care, eye tests and medicines
- education is free for all school-children
- special rules apply to the arrest, questioning and punishment of children accused of breaking the law.

Both Wales and Scotland have decided that children need a person to look after and speak up for their rights. In Scotland this person is called the Children's Commissioner. He or she speaks up for children and investigates cases where children's rights may not have been respected.

The United Kingdom has signed up to the European Convention on Human Rights. This set of laws changed the way that young people may be punished in school. They also gave children the right to be consulted on some issues. This includes issues on education and family life.

Almost all countries in the world belong to the United Nations Organisation. It has a similar agreement that most member countries have signed, agreeing to respect everyone's Human Rights and also the Rights of the Child.

Activities:

1. Look at the poster on page 37 and write down ten rights that are included in the UN agreement on the Rights of the Child.

2. Which of these rights do you think is the most important to you? Give a reason for your answer.

The UN Convention gives Rights and Protection to Children

Shelter

Education

Health Care

Living Standards

Worldwide Rights for and Protection of Children

Family Life

Emergency Care

Nationality

Freedom of Speech

Freedom from Torture & Unlawful Arrest

Participate in Decisions

Extension:

Find out about the ways that some of these rights are not met for children around the world (e.g. Afghanistan, Algeria, China, Sierra Leone, South Africa, Turkey).

What ways are suggested to help young people have a better life in these countries?

You might use websites like those below:

http://www.unicef.org/action/programmes
http://www.comicrelief.org.uk
http://www.oxfam.org.uk/coolplanet/ontheline/
http://www.sciaf.org.uk
http://www.christianaid.org.uk

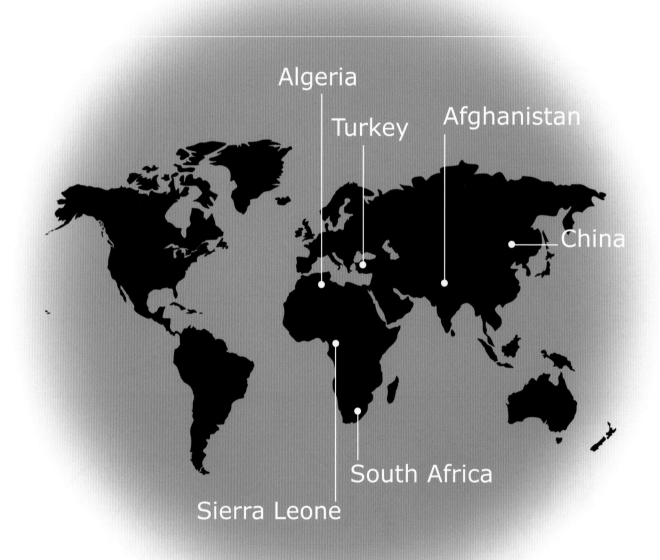

Rules, Rights and Responsibilities: Vandalism and You

Linview people are very proud of their local community. Local businesses give money to buy bulbs and other plants for the flower beds, planters and hanging baskets on the main street. In summer, many people spend a lot of time planting and watering the pots and planters around the town.

It is early August. The town is expecting the judges for the 'Scotland in Bloom' competition to arrive on Friday morning. On Wednesday, the people on their way to work find the bus shelter has been damaged. All the flowerbeds nearby have been trampled.

A person passing by comments:

I bet it was teenagers from the school who did this. Young people have no respect for other people's property. Whoever did this should be punished.

Activities:

1. Suggest the groups of people in Linview who might be upset by this damage.

2. Why might many people in the town be angry?

3. Do you agree with this man's view? Does he have any evidence for what he says?

4. Do you think that Anna and Scott would agree with him?
   Give a reason for your answer.

Sometimes a person is caught by the police and accused of doing such damage. Possible punishments might be a fine or a period of hours spent on community service. This might involve repairing the damage caused or working in another way to help the community such as cutting grass, painting a fence or even giving football lessons. Only for very serious damage or a long series of offences would imprisonment be used as the punishment.

School vandals cause

£200,000 damage

A t Hailesland Primary School in Edinburgh, vandals broke in one night last week. They broke windows and doors and even wrecked the school's computer suite.

They poured water over the computers and smashed their screens. Police suspect a local gang of children, aged between 12 and 14, of causing the damage.

They said that the people who did the damage were "very cheeky". They'd used the school's own camera to take photographs of the scene 'before' and 'after' their visit.

August 2002

EXTRA! **The News** EXTRA!

5. Which offences should get:
   – the lightest punishment?
   – the most severe punishment?
   Explain your reason for this view.

6. What would you need to be certain of before any person was punished?

7. What do you think would be a good punishment for the kind of vandalism in Linview? Give reasons for your answer.

8. Although vandalism is annoying and this example made the town unsightly, the damage was minor. Read the news clipping above about a serious case of vandalism.

a. Briefly describe what happened at Hailesland Primary School one night in August 2002.

b. How do you think the following people from around this school would probably feel about the damage:
   – Pupils?
   – Parents?
   – Teachers and the local council?

c. Who were suspected by police of doing this?

d. What evidence did the police have?

e. In your view what kind of punishment would be best for anyone found guilty of this kind of damage?

Rules, Rights and Responsibilities: Young People and the Law

If young people are suspected of serious vandalism, or any other law-breaking activity, then they may be arrested and questioned by the police. In most cases a parent or another adult who is not in the police must be present when they are questioned. Some young people cannot be questioned at all because they are too young or have learning difficulties.

There are important differences between how children are treated in the legal systems of Scotland and England. In Scotland, young people over the age of 8 years are expected to know the difference between right and wrong. (This is called the age of responsibility.) In England the age of responsibility is at 10 years.

However, if young people have got into trouble with the police, they will be treated in a different way from adults in both countries. In some cases, their parents will be held to be responsible and may be required to go on a course to learn how to deal with bad behaviour in young children.

 Activities:

1. Do you agree that a child aged 8 (or 10) knows the difference between right and wrong?

2. Should young people who break the law be treated differently from adults?

3. Is it a parent's responsibility when a young child behaves badly and breaks the law? Explain your view.

Rules, Rights and Responsibilities: The Children's Panel

In England, young offenders are usually warned by the police first. If they are caught again, young people under 18 may be brought before a youth court. This court is made up of three people called magistrates who are not lawyers. They judge (or decide on) the evidence for the case. The court meets separately from an adult court.

If the young person is found guilty, the court can decide on a caution, a supervision order, or a fine; or it can order attendance on Saturdays at a centre. In very serious cases, they may send children over 12 to a secure unit. Offenders over 15 can be sent to a young offenders institution.

In Scotland, it is very unusual for a child over the age of 8 but under 16 to appear in court. Instead, the child is brought before the Children's Panel. The Panel is made up of three local people. The Reporter (sometimes a lawyer) is in charge.

The Reporter receives information from the child's school, social workers and the police. The Panel can decide to take no action or to introduce a supervision order. This means that the child is either placed under the care of a relative or is supervised at home by a social worker. Alternatively, the child may be placed in foster care or in a residential home.

Activities:

1. Draw up a table like the one below and complete it using the information from the text:

Treatment	England	Scotland
Age a child should know right from wrong		
Where a case is heard		
How many people decide?		
Is a guilty verdict possible?		
Possible outcomes		

2. Look at the information below in Sources 1, 2 and 3.

> SOURCE 1: One in every forty youngsters aged 16 and one in every twelve young people aged 17 is convicted of a crime. In addition, Children's Panels deal with more than 13,000 children who have committed at least three crimes each.

SOURCE 2

Youth offences

year	youth offences (000)
2000	13,723
1999	14,003
1976	15,413

0   13   14   15   16
youth offences (000)

SOURCE 3

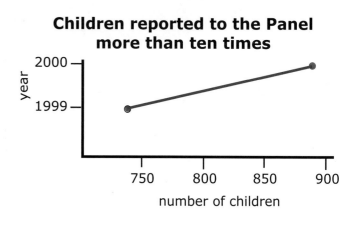

Children reported to the Panel more than ten times

Tom Wood, Deputy Chief Constable of the Lothian and Borders Police Force, said:

> "Youth crime is not on the increase".

Do you agree with Tom Wood? Explain your answer.

Rules, Rights and Responsibilities: **The Law and You**

"Today in England, a mother was sent to prison for 28 days for not sending her two children to school. The girls are aged 14 and 15. The council had tried for the last two years to get the children to go to school each day. A taxi was even provided for the girls to get to school on time, but it made no difference. The girls usually went straight back home.

The judge criticised the mother for failing to make sure the girls went to school as the law required until they were aged 16. "No matter what the problems at home, the girls have a right to education and that is what matters," she said. Their 24-year-old sister took them back to her home while their mother was taken off to prison.

Activities:

Read the news story above then answer the questions below.

1. Why was the mother sent to prison?

2. In what way was she breaking the law?

3. What ages were the children?

4. How had the council tried to get the girls to go to school?

5. Do you agree with what the judge
   – said about the girls' right to education?
   – gave as the punishment?

6. What other punishments would you consider for:
   – the parents of such truants?
   – the truants themselves?

People in Society: Citizenship

At Linview Primary, the Pupils' Council suggests to Mr Brown that the school should have an award each month for one pupil who has set an example by being a 'good citizen'. This not only means working hard in class, but also helping others in the year group in school and working for the community outside school.

Scott is very embarrassed to discover at assembly that he is called on to collect an award. Mr Brown explains that the teachers and pupils in his class suggested his name because of his work for the Pupils' Council. He has attended every meeting and makes sure his class knows what has been discussed. He is also praised for the Tidy Up Linview Campaign in town. Scott receives a certificate and a CD voucher.

He is very proud when he goes home and shows his parents and his Gran.

Well Scott what a nice surprise!

That's my boy. Good at football and a social conscience. I hope this doesn't mean you want to deliver leaflets so you can be an MSP in future.

We're all very proud of you.

Did you know that twice each year there are awards from the Queen for adults who have been good citizens? Susan at the lunch club got an MBE for all the voluntary work she does with us oldies.

Bill, the janitor at Scott's primary school, got one for helping with the football teams for more than 20 years.

You need to do a lot more than just your normal job, of course. You never know, you two, when you're older you might get one too!

Activities:

1. Do you think Scott deserved the school's 'Good Citizen' award? Give reasons for your answer.

2. Do you think your school should have an award like this? Explain your view.

3. How would you and your class decide who should get such an award?

4. Bill and Susan got MBEs from the Queen for helping people in their local communities. Do you agree that people should get an award for this kind of work?

5. Is there someone in your local community whom you think deserves an award for Good Citizenship?   Explain your answer.